INSPIRED:

How to Write a "Must-Read" Memoir

A Step-by-Step Guide and Workbook

By Celeste Chin and Kris Pfeifer

Copyright ©2024. By Celeste Chin and Kris Pfeifer. All rights reserved. No part of this book may be reproduced in any form or by any electronic or mechanical means without written permission from the authors, except by a reviewer who may quote the text for purposes of review.

Library of Congress Cataloging-in-Publication Data has been applied for.

ISBN: 978-1-7334929-4-2

Limit of Liability Disclaimer of Warranty: While the publisher and authors have used their best efforts in preparing this book, they make no representations or warranties with respect to the accuracy and completeness of the contents of this book and specifically disclaim any implied warranties of merchantability or fitness for a particular purpose. The advice and strategies contained herein may not be suitable for your situation. The information in this book should not be considered personal writing or publishing advice. You should consult with a professional for your specific needs where appropriate. There is no guarantee, either written or implied, regarding publication of your work.

Table of Contents

About Us 4

A General Overview: The Memoir Basics 6

The Lesson Index 9

Lesson One: Establishing a Foundation 10

Lesson Two: Information Collection 18

Lesson Three: Create an Outline 24

Lesson Four: Establish Your Writing Style 30

Lesson Five: Begin Writing 33

Lesson Six: Self Edit 40

Bonus: Unstuck Yourself! 44

Memoir Recommendations 47

About Us...

Celeste Chin

Celeste is the founder and chief ghostwriter for Creative License Publishing (CLP). She has found a unique way to help writers in today's, sometimes complicated, publishing world. Celeste works across all genres to help writers mirror the quality of mainstream publishers while maintaining their fresh, innovative ideas for the reading public.

Kris Pfeifer

Kris is a graphic designer, and the creative mind behind Pfeifer Design studio. With a passion for merging design and storytelling, she specializes in creating captivating book layouts and covers for self-published authors. Using a personalized and collaborative approach, Kris works closely with authors to bring their unique ideas to life visually–designing layouts that immerse readers in each narrative while crafting covers that serve as a compelling gateway to the world within the pages.

Together, Kris and Celeste founded the self-publishing arm of CLP. Since its inception in 2019, they have served a wide variety of clients with their publishing needs, ranging from ghostwriting, beta reads, edits, proofreads, cover design, layout, and uploading to on-demand distribution sites. Many of the authors they've assisted have written on topics such as business, psychology, self-help, and memoirs. Kris and Celeste have developed a passion for working with clients to bring their unique stories to life and fulfill their goals of writing their memoirs.

But what they've uncovered in the process is a method to help each memoir writer deliver their incredible stories in the most captivating way to take their readers on a page-turning journey.

Dear Writer,

Ready to write your memoir?! We can only assume that you experienced and survived challenging, beautiful, emotional, sad, humorous, or frustrating times that resulted in learning and emotional growth. Or you have heard the words, "You need to write a book!" Whatever the reason for writing your memoir, understand that creating a "must-read" is more than having a story to tell. It's about how you deliver that story.

But don't worry, that's why we are here. In this book, we will guide you through every step of writing your memoir to capture and keep your reader from beginning to end. Having ghostwritten, consulted on, edited, and self-published many memoirs, we've isolated the critical attributes of a "must-read" and designed a foolproof method to ensure your story delivers from start to finish.

First, as your writing guides, we must express our excitement that you've picked up this book, as it speaks volumes about your commitment to producing a page-turning memoir. And second, we acknowledge your courage and determination because this journey won't be easy. The process will be a rollercoaster of emotions as you uncover joyful, trying, funny, and possibly painful memories. Therefore, we encourage you to allow yourself ample grace, kindness, and understanding throughout.

As you work through each step, we hope you reach out to us if you have any questions, are struggling with specific tasks, or need more personal assistance. All you need to do is go to the link provided to contact us. You will also receive a free initial personal consultation, during which we will discuss your potential needs, answer any questions, and/or provide guidance.

So, let's get started!

Celeste and Kris

A General Overview
The Memoir Basics

Let us share with you a story of two authors we worked with:

Author number one had been abused as a child and turned to drugs as a means of coping. His story, in some ways, was as old as time. But what made it unique was the author's approach. He told about his days living on the streets and the crimes he committed to feed his drug habit–sharing profound revelations about himself. Then, he took the reader through the blood, sweat, and determination needed to turn his life around, get clean, and focus on helping rehabilitate addicts like himself. Ultimately, his story made you cry, question, and ultimately cheer this underdog on to victory.

Author number one had written a **"must-read"** manuscript.

Author number two had similar difficult moments in his life. He grew up poor; his father left the family broke. He endured an abusive stepfather and an alcoholic mother. This man never felt loved and grew up floundering for years, making poor choices in an attempt to fill himself up emotionally through sex and alcohol. Eventually, he was forced to find the right path or face the possibility of being homeless. However, author number two was guarded and unwilling to visit the depths of his despair. Unlike author number one, he didn't want to reveal his inappropriate and disastrous choices that nearly destroyed his life. Instead, he chose to sugarcoat his memoir to save himself and his family from embarrassment.

Ultimately, author number one's story read far better than two. Why? Not because one's experiences were more sensational or impactful than the other. But simply because of author number one's willingness to be open and honest about his past.

Therefore, these examples beg the question:

Are you ready to get real and write a "must-read" memoir?

If you've gotten this far, we suspect the answer is yes! So, keep author number one in your head, and know if he can do it with our help, so can you!

Here's an essential truth: Writing a memoir can be a fun, cathartic, emotional, frustrating, and exhausting experience all rolled into one giant ball. And as you pour through your notes, pictures, videos, and mementos and talk to family and friends, you may feel the magnitude of the overall endeavor; it's expected. Don't worry; it's why we've created this step-by-step guide. Our process will keep you organized, focused, and clear on your message.

By now, you've noticed we use the term "must-read" often. The reason is it refers to the magnitude to which your writing draws the readers in, hooks them from the start, and keeps them engaged to where they can't put your book down. Your primary objective is for your story to be written precisely in this manner: capturing and keeping the reader's interest from start to finish.

> To achieve that ultimate goal, let us introduce **the four main objectives of a "must-read" memoir:**
>
> 1. Know Your Target Reader – Know Your Target Audience
> 2. Have A Clear Theme – A Point or Message
> 3. Make it Real – Be Honest, Do Not Sugarcoat
> 4. Write Like It's a Novel – More Showing than Telling

What do we mean by knowing your target reader? If you want to sell your memoir, the information you share must be pertinent to those interested in your story. Why? Because you want the reader to create a connection to the content to ignite their interest. For example, if you are writing a memoir about your life as a plastic surgeon in Hollywood, your primary target audience will most likely be adult females, many in their mid-life. Because, statistically speaking, those are the individuals who get the most plastic surgery. Therefore, given your audience, you might integrate patient stories your reader can identify with—an essential component for establishing and maintaining engagement.

A theme or message must emanate from your story—memoirs often convey a struggle, difficulty, or something learned. Some frequent themes encompass travel, adventure, family, romance, career, spirituality, grief, addictions, mental illness, and so on.

Your third goal should be to make it real. Be open and honest about each part of your story. Avoid hiding facts or glossing over events. Often, writers will gloss over a particular part to try and portray themselves in a better light. To facilitate a reader's connection, they must see your failures, shortcomings, and successes—humanize yourself. Your readers aren't perfect, so they will relate to you more if they see themselves in you.

Lastly, and probably the most crucial objective, is to write your memoir like it's a novel. Here are the following elements that must be present to achieve this goal:

- **Write in the first person.** This is your story, so it should read from your point of view and sound like you.
- **Get to the good stuff quick.** Create a hook to start and engross the reader in your journey.
- **Keep the pace going.** Do not provide unnecessary details (details that don't add to or support the story) that drag the story out or distract the reader from the theme.
- **Show, don't tell.** Showing versus telling refers to constantly explaining to the reader what happened. Showing involves describing scenes with dialogue, for example, to demonstrate a point or a significant event.

Throughout the book, we will go into much greater detail on these objectives. The following pages will provide easy-to-follow, detailed lessons and assignments to take you step-by-step through writing a captivating and informative memoir. But you cannot skip any step!

If you need any consultation, scan the QR code below, that goes to our website contact form, and we will help.

You may work on the assignments in each lesson in your own journal or notebook, on your computer, or we have provided space within this workbook for you to make notes. Whatever works best for you!

The Lesson Index

Each lesson builds on the one before and will consist of the following:

- A discussion where the topic is explained.
- An assignment portion designed as a building block toward the final product.

You must not skip any lesson or any of the assignments associated with them. Trust the process!

- ☐ Lesson One: **Establishing a Foundation** 16
- ☐ Lesson Two: **Information Collection** 18
- ☐ Lesson Three: **Create an Outline** 24
- ☐ Lesson Four: **Establish Your Writing Style** 30
- ☐ Lesson Five: **Begin Writing** 33
- ☐ Lesson Six: **Self-Edit** 40

Lesson One
Establishing a Foundation

Below, author Adrienne Brodeur, who penned one of our favorite memoirs, brilliantly describes the basis of any memoir:

> "*Wild Game* does not pretend to tell the whole story—years have been compressed into sentences, friends and lovers edited out, details scrubbed. Time has scattered particulars. What follows in these pages are recollections, interpretations, and renderings of moments that shaped my life, all subject to perspective, persuasion, and longing." – Adrienne Brodeur

OBJECTIVE
To determine the answers to the following:

Memoirs are not about telling someone's life story but about telling a story within one's life focused on a specific objective or theme. So, the first lesson addresses establishing a foundation by identifying the main objectives:

- **Defining Memoirs.** Determining if you wish to write a memoir.
- **Theme.** The message you wish to convey.
- **Motivation.** Why you want to write a memoir.
- **Target Market.** Who you are writing it for.
- **Goals.** The end objective.

Defining Memoirs

Often, individuals use the words autobiography, biography, and memoir interchangeably. However, they are distinct genres. Please read the definitions below:

- A memoir relays a memory or series of memories about an experience. There is a focus on a specific theme, where the writer might convey a difficulty they overcame and a lesson(s) learned, for example. A memoir could encompass travel, adventure, family, romance, career, spirituality, grief, addictions, mental illness, etc.
- An autobiography (first person) or biography (third person) is when you or someone else writes about what happens over the subject's lifespan, from birth to the present day.

If you are satisfied, that your story meets the definition of a memoir, then continue.

Theme

The theme of your memoir is the message you wish to send to the reader. For example, we previously talked about a client we referred to as "author number one" who overcame a drug addiction. This author had lived on the streets, endured horrific conditions, and participated in criminal behavior. He has since turned his life around and is a productive member of society. And he wanted his story to inspire others to get their lives on track. Thus, he chose his message to center around the power of perseverance: never giving up.

There are several elements associated with defining your theme:

- **Relatability**. Your theme is unique already because it's yours. Still, it should be something others can relate to their own situations, such as overcoming adversity, fighting for independence, or living through abuse.
- **Capture and Keep.** Your theme must acquire and hold the potential reader's interest from beginning to end.
- **Clarity.** The theme should be clearly understood by the reader. If the reader fails to identify the message or is confused by your stance on the content, you will lose them and/or fail to achieve your goal.

To ensure relatability and the ability to interest your readers, we suggest going to the bookstore or searching online for other memoirs with similar themes. This will assure you that people can and desire to connect to your topic—if books are selling, then there's interest.

Capturing, keeping, and effectively relaying your theme will happen as you write. If you follow the instructions in this book, you will achieve these desired elements of your theme.

Motivations

Our actions are a result of our motivations. Humans do things for specific reasons, whether they acknowledge them or not. Writing a memoir can be an emotional event for some and fun and light for others, but you need to be honest about why you are taking this journey before you can approach how you will write your story.

Why is this necessary?

Because *why* you desire to write a memoir will impact *how* you write it. For example, we had a client who lost her husband. She wrote about her grieving process, but her desire was to be an inspiration to others mourning a loss. So yes, the writing process provoked many tears, but her story was delivered with positivity and encouragement.

Below are some of the popular reasons why you may write a memoir:

- Catharsis
- Revenge (We do not recommend writing a memoir for this reason)
- Teach/inform
- Inspire
- Share
- Legacy
- Set the record straight
- Shock
- Entertain/humor
- Vindication

Note the above reasons may or may not exemplify your reasons for writing. So take the time to think and be honest with yourself.

Target Market

This encompasses who you will be writing the book for. Ask yourself: Who do I see buying this book? Who do I want to read this book? Identifying multiple markets is not uncommon, yet one typically prevails over the other. The predominant market is defined as your "primary target market."

We will use an example to further explain how to define your target market(s): Let's pretend you are writing a memoir about growing up with an alcoholic mother. Your theme concerns overcoming adversity and persevering as an adult despite a challenging upbringing. And your motivation is to share your story to inspire others who experienced difficult childhoods at the hands of their parents and for personal cathartic reasons.

Given the above foundation, your primary market would be adults (identify age range if possible) with similar experiences with drug or alcohol-dependent parents or those who may have experienced difficult childhoods because of parental neglect or abuse.

However, there are many readers who love memoirs and might find the topic interesting without having any experiences even remotely close to the author. This group will tend to be smaller and is considered your "secondary market."

When assessing your target market(s), you will also want to see what other similar books are already published and who their readers are. You can do this through a simple search on Google and/or even Amazon (some of this you should have already from when you researched for relatability). Also, knowing your genre and the market for your topic will help if your goals are around sales and being traditionally published. So, do your research!

Goals

To determine your overall or end goal, ask yourself: What will a successful memoir mean to me once my manuscript is complete? For some, it may be to complete the manuscript and put it in their closet. Others may have goals of a bestseller or to be traditionally published.

Your goals are not typically the same as your motive because the motive is what compelled you to put pen to paper or fingers on the keyboard. Whereas your end goal is what you hope to achieve once the work is completed in terms of publication and impact. Some may have blurred lines between motive and goals, but more times than not, they are separate.

Below are some potential goals:

- Story to be published
- Bestseller
- Self-publish
- Traditionally published
- Publish for family and loved ones only
- Use as supplementary lecture material
- Legacy – to document for future generations
- To build a brand; self-promotion

Your goal(s) may not be on the list or could be several listed. They are what they are, and it's essential to write them down, which you will do in the assignment section. The reason for establishing a defined goal is twofold:

1. **Create a reference point for yourself throughout the writing process to measure your progress and create accountability.**

2. **To create a reference point when incorporating specific elements, which we will discuss in lesson four.**

For example, if your only goal is to build a brand, you must write a memoir with a theme consistent with your created brand. Suppose your brand is focused on painting as a means of self-expression and therapy because you've experienced its healing powers. Therefore, you might talk about how art therapy saved you or someone you loved, for example. The two parts, theme and goal, should be in alignment.

But if, for example, your goal is to write just for your family, then you may or may not want to include some information. We had a client who wanted to share how she recovered from her divorce and found love again. But there were specific facts she didn't want to disclose because they would be hurtful to her daughters. So, knowing her end objective helped her determine what she included in her manuscript.

Therefore, knowing your goals will help produce accountability and focus.

You will hear us often say that you can't publish a book if you don't finish writing it. Or look at it this way: Your grandkids won't know how you built an empire if you don't finish writing your story. Essentially, you can't motivate or inspire others with a half-done memoir that stays in your closet!

You get the point: Set your goals and achieve them one step at a time.

Summary

This initial stage in your memoir will be the foundation from which you build your story. If you don't already know, writing anything can begin one way and go off course without you noticing. But if you have clearly defined guidelines and use them to check yourself, you will have created a solid base to work from so that even if you veer off course, you can get back on track quickly.

We had a client whose memoir, according to them, was seventy-five percent complete, and they wished for us to finish it. The problems unfolded right away because they had unclear goals. They never took the time to do the steps we just described. They just sat down and wrote until they got "stuck." Therefore, as we reviewed the completed portion of the manuscript, we noted the lack of clear messaging or theme, and the story droned on without purpose.

The client didn't want to hear this diagnosis and refused to fix it. The memoir, sadly, remains incomplete to this day. We wish this were a rare case, but unfortunately, this is far more common than the person who completes and publishes their memoir. Yes, it's why we've written this workbook!

So let that story be a cautionary tale and a motivator to keep you moving forward!

You've got this!

 **LESSON 1 ASSIGNMENTS:**

1. **Are you writing a memoir?** Remember, the definition of a memoir is as follows:

   A memoir relays a memory or memories of an experience you want to share. There is a focus on a theme, where the writer conveys a difficulty they overcame and the lesson learned, for example. A memoir might encompass travel, adventure, family, romance, career, spirituality, grief, addictions, mental illness, etc. A memoir is not a compilation of every aspect of your life from birth to the present.

   ☐ If your answer is yes, then continue to number 2.

2. **What is your theme?**

   Below, define your theme. Yet think about how you will achieve the above elements of theme: relatability, capture and keep, and clarity. For example, let's assume you are writing a memoir about overcoming a disability. You might write in this assignment:

   The theme is about perseverance despite setbacks I hadn't planned on. I will relay the journey I took learning to live with MS. It's relatable because millions are diagnosed with and suffer from MS. The theme will capture and keep the reader's interest through a clear and honest depiction of the negatives of the disease and the surprising positives I didn't anticipate.

   Make sure you hit the following points:

   ☐ Clarity – is your message clear and understandable?
   ☐ Relatability – would a reader be able to relate to your message?
   ☐ Capture and Keep – will your message interest readers?

On the lines below, write the **motivation(s) behind your memoir.** There may be more than one reason. They can be anything you feel, such as one of the following:

- ☐ Catharsis
- ☐ Revenge
- ☐ Teach/inform
- ☐ Inspire
- ☐ Share
- ☐ Legacy
- ☐ Set the record straight
- ☐ Shock
- ☐ Entertain/humor
- ☐ Vindication
- ☐ Other

Be sure to be transparent and honest:

_____
_____
_____
_____
_____
_____
_____
_____

Who is your target market? (review definition on pg 14 if needed)

Primary:

_____
_____
_____
_____
_____
_____
_____
_____

Secondary:

_____
_____
_____
_____
_____
_____

Please write your *overall goal for your memoir*, knowing you may have more than one: Here are the examples shown previously:

- ☐ Story to be published
- ☐ Bestseller
- ☐ Self-publish
- ☐ Traditionally published
- ☐ Publish for family and loved ones only
- ☐ Use as supplementary lecture material
- ☐ Legacy – to document for future generations
- ☐ To build a brand; self-promotion
- ☐ Other

_____
_____
_____
_____
_____
_____
_____
_____
_____
_____
_____
_____
_____

Lesson Two
Information Collection

> "I never wrote things down to remember; I always wrote things down so I could forget... Recently, I worked up the courage to sit down with those diaries and have a look at the thirty-five years of writing about who I've been over the last fifty. And you know what? I enjoyed myself more than I thought I would. I laughed, I cried, I realized I had remembered more than I expected, and forgot less." Matthew McConaughey – *Greenlights*

 OBJECTIVE:
To gather all the relevant and accurate data to support the goal and theme of the memoir

The next step for you in the process is to **research yourself**. Yes, it's time to dive back into the memories you packed away, either in your brain, journals, photo albums, or mementos you never threw out because they meant far more than the item would ever be worth—that movie ticket stub that marked the night you met your wife or the bracelet you got from your mom on your high school graduation. It's time to start digging, dear writers, and brush off the cobwebs of your memories.

For those who cook, skipping this step will be like making a meal or baking without all the necessary ingredients. And we all know how that ends! So, do not skip this step and begin typing away from memory; no matter how good you think your memory is, you risk leaving out an important part(s).

This step is about compiling and analyzing your content from a systematic and organized approach:

Step 1 – Collection:

- **Take notes.** Write down anything you can think of relating to your experience(s). Use this workbook, a pad of paper, or your computer to create a list of bullet points you wish to cover. If you only have general ideas at this time, that's fine.
- **Memory recall.** Use photos and personal items to spark memories and feelings. For each picture or item, write down any information you recall, including emotions: how you feel when looking at the pictures or objects, what your feelings were when you took the picture, or what the object represented for you. Be as open and honest as possible. Use

all five senses as a guide when describing your feelings.
- **Interview.** Interview family or friends to help your memory or gain a different perspective. Keep notes of what your interviews reveal, and ask if your family and friends also have pictures to help you.

Step 2 – Organize and Analyze:

- **Compile and assess.**
  - Review all the notes and decide what information you want to include. What supports your message (theme)? Any content that doesn't move your story forward or serve the theme should be eliminated from your compilation of potential content.
  - Add any additional details that come to mind in the process. We recommend doing this step with marked intervals for recall. For example, what you may have forgotten on Monday morning may be clear that afternoon. So, list, jot down, and revisit a few times before you complete your data collection.

- **Review/Identify hook.** Read your notes to find the element to hook the reader, and write that down.

Before we explain how to identify the hook, let's define the meaning: *A hook is your ability to get that reader interested from the start and keep them reading.* You will create one at the beginning of the book and drop several throughout to keep the reader's interest piqued. We will get into the specifics of how later on. But for this initial review of your notes, try to find something that will be impactful to the reader.

For example, memoirs are often linear in how they are written; a lot of "this happened, then that happened" in order of events. It's also why many fail because they drone on without ever laying the groundwork to hook a reader and maintain their desire for answers. So when our client came to us with an inspirational and poignant memoir involving racism, we assessed his notes carefully to find that vital moment to set the tone and hook the reader immediately. Right away, we placed the reader in a board meeting before a big merger that would propel him forward or start him back at square one. We left a question (hook) firmly planted in the reader's mind without delivering the resolution as we delved back into the history of how the author got to that point in the first place. Once we had our carrot dangled in front of the reader, we knew how to lay out the story with twists and turns, dropping some additional small hooks to keep that reader even more interested.

So, during this investigative and collection process, highlight potential hooks. You may have several points that will grab the reader. If you do, all the better because you want more than one to sprinkle throughout. You can decipher which one you use initially as we continue through the process.

If you are still unsure, we always tell our writers to think about a book they loved and couldn't put down or their favorite television series or movie. Then, to ask themselves: What first got me and had me wanting more? What was it about the story that had you saying, "I can't walk away yet; I have to find out....?"

- **Timeline.** Know the timeline of events for factual purposes so that you don't confuse the reader. But knowing the timeline isn't because you necessarily will write in that order. As we said in the previous point, individuals often write their memoirs in a very linear format. Sometimes, it works well, and others can leave the story flat.

- **Tone.** Determine voice/tone and how you will sound to the reader. Again, revisit your motives, goals, and target market to help determine how you wish to sound.

The tone is how your voice will be interpreted by the reader. First, you will want the tone to reflect your personality because memoirs are personal, if nothing else. Second, the tone should follow the theme or message you wish to promote. For example, suppose you are writing a memoir about losing your job and how humor affected your perseverance. Then, you may want your tone to be a contrast of difficult times against a self-deprecating humoristic approach. However, if losing your job and finding another one took you through serious, dark times, your tone would be more somber.

Summary

We've worked with many clients who have failed to do the previous steps and found during our edits that they missed things, their facts didn't line up, or they could have started with a better hook. This created extensive rewrites.

So, take your time collecting and analyzing because it will make or break your outline, which we will cover next!

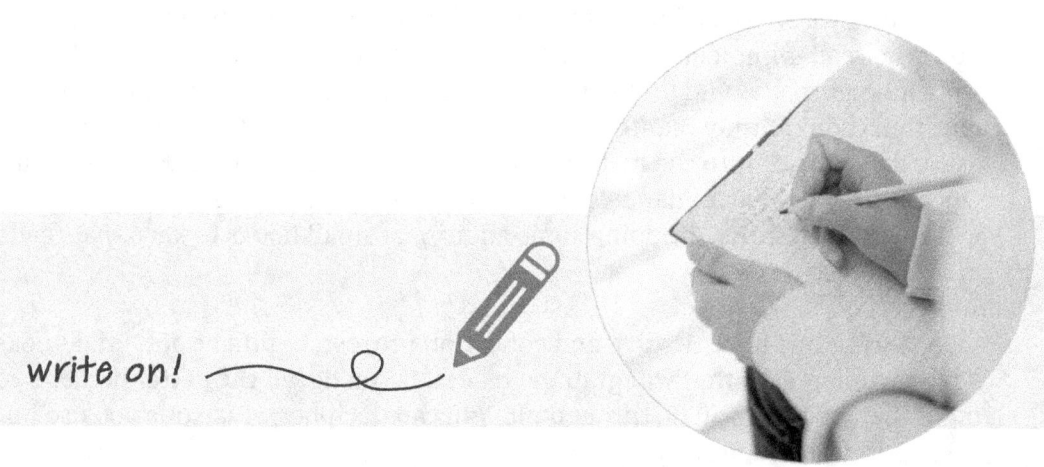

write on!

LESSON TWO ASSIGNMENT:

Complete the following steps:

1. **In bullet point form, list the points, events, conversations, and such you wish to cover in your memoir. Delineating the timeline of what happened and when.**

2. **Highlight what your initial hook will be. You may find one or several potential hooks.**

3. **What will your tone be?**

Additional Notes:

Lesson Three
Create an Outline

"Normally, I spend a week on the outline and take two weeks to write the book." - R. L. Stine

 OBJECTIVE: To create structure and a basis for accountability

Outlines make some individuals squirm or break out in hives as they have flashbacks to high school English. Trust us, you will not be judged on your outline, but the tighter and more detailed you are, the easier the writing will flow. For example, a good outline should provide the following:

- **Completeness** - A comprehensive outline makes sure you encompass all your points.
- **Accountability** – An outline supports you in staying on track with your goals because you are more apt to achieve them when you write them down.
- **Focus** - The outline will keep you on point and focused. One of the biggest obstacles to publication is finishing the work. There are many reasons for this, but getting "off-track" is a real problem, and you can't get back "on-track" easily without a "track" to begin with.

Think of the outline as your memoir roadmap, without which you will get lost, take circuitous routes, and lose time and perspective. For those who can't drive without Google Maps, start seeing this tool as your navigation system for your memoir.

Your outline should sketch your memoir from the introduction to the final chapter. Be sure to include each chapter's points to be covered and specific memories to be conveyed. It will also be where you write down the foundation points from lesson one so you will always have them next to you as a reminder.

Below is an example of a detailed outline to help you construct yours. But don't get caught up in the form; it is about having your "foundation" (lesson one) and ideas down (lesson two) in an easy-to-follow format with clearly defined timelines to complete (lesson three).

Setting Realistic Goals

Once your outline is complete regarding chapters and content, you will want to go back and establish writing goals regarding completion dates for each drafted chapter. These dates are for the rough copy completion, not the edited version, although once you've completed the draft of the entire manuscript, you can go back and add dates for your self-edit. Due dates, even those self-imposed, encourage accountability and motivation; every time you fulfill one, you'll find more incentive to move to the next.

When we write for personal reasons, we answer to ourselves to make it to the finish line. Well, we all know that can make for fluid deadlines. This goes for most of us, so it's not a judgment but a recognition of a fact that can be mitigated by using the outline to hold your feet to the fire.

Yet, the goals established should be within reach and doable. If you estimate it will take two hours to draft a chapter, we recommend doubling that time and adding an hour. Why? Because through years of experience, what you think will progress in short order often takes *at least* twice as long.

We recently had a client writing her memoir who called us to say she would have the draft ready for us to edit in a few days. Two and a half weeks later, we received another call from her, expressing frustration that the process took her so long!

Our point: It always takes longer than you think, so use our rule of thumb when setting your goals.

How to Use Your Outline

Once you've completed your outline and reviewed it, of course, you will begin the process of writing, which we will detail in the next chapter. But it's critical to understand that the outline you've put together is not just to help you get started. In fact, you will use it again and again, but specifically, during the writing process, you will use it as follows:

- You will review the outline before writing each chapter to provide focus.
- You may review the outline while writing your draft if you need to regain your thoughts and remind yourself of the goals for the chapter you are working on.
- You will review the outline after each draft to ensure completeness in accounting for each intended topic.

OUTLINE - SAMPLE

Memoir: Title to Be Determined
Objective/Theme: To share a personal experience with grief, to inspire others mourning the loss of a loved one.
Memoir Goals in Publication: Self-publication, traditionally published, or printed for family only
Draft Completion date: XXX
Pages: Approximately 100 pages
Target Market: Primary: Adults – specifically those dealing with grief issues or knowing someone coping with a loss. Secondary: Adults interested in memoirs addressing triumph over adversity
Additional items: Include inspirational quotes at the beginning of each chapter

Outline Details

I. **Introduction** – The reader will learn about the author and the reason for writing the book. It's the first chance for the author to connect with the reader.

   Complete on _____

   A. Begin by introducing the subject matter by asking the reader a question. The question should make the reader think about their own struggles and hint at the author's current life and challenges.

   B. Quick overview of the author's life, talk about dreams and how the author always imagined life would go.

   C. Allude to there being a tragedy the author had to overcome to heighten the interest.

II. **Chapter One** – Memoirs must have a theme, so the author must hit that theme immediately while capturing the reader's interest. The theme will be "healing after a loss."

   Complete on _____

   A. Open with a hook – ***. This scene will put the reader into healing challenges without spelling them out yet – capture the reader's interest from the start.

   B. Share the anguish over the hooking scene (anger/guilt).

C. Introduce the family dynamic to the reader.
D. As the author grapples with her own emotions, show how the author struggles with the memories of the past:
   1. Dreams on ***
   2. Meeting ****
   3. Dreams of ***

II to IX. Chapters Two through Nine – Continue to give glimpses into the life before the tragedy contrasted against the severe pain of loss. You want the reader to connect with the author and her loss so they can feel the depths of despair.

Complete on _____

A. Stories that support the theme and allow the reader to go through the peaks and valleys. Be raw and real about the events.

III. Concluding Chapter…author's thoughts…This sums up the author's experience and should include some ideas for others to consider as they heal from their pain. Perhaps at the end of the book, give names and numbers of places to reach out to in times of grief.

Complete on _____

A. Things the author would have done differently and lessons learned.
B. What the author learned.
C. What the author learned about others in her life.
D. Advice the author has for others.

 LESSON THREE ASSIGNMENT:

The prior assignments will now come into play as you construct the outline. Follow the steps below:

1. **Review the sample outline from a published memoir on loss and recovery.**
2. **Gather your information on goals, objectives, themes, and target market (lesson one).**
3. **Review your bullet points and finalize the hook you will open with (lesson two).**
4. **Use the space on the next page to begin writing your outline.**

Think of the outline as your memoir roadmap.

Remember to establish writing goals regarding completion dates for each drafted chapter!

Lesson Four
Establish Your Writing Style

> "Setting goals is the first step in turning the invisible into the visible."
> - Tony Robbins

 OBJECTIVE: To determine an effective process to write your memoir—answering where, when, and how.

If you completed the outline from the prior assignment, congratulations! If not, go back and do it! Skipping the outlining process will result in a memoir that lacks focus and falls short of all its goals. Remember, you don't have to create one precisely like the sample, but the document should spell out every detail displayed on the sample. Your outline will be your go-to tool in the writing process—the map to your destination.

Once you've completed all the prior steps, should you sit down and start typing away? Yes, you can, but if you're not a seasoned writer, we don't recommend it. Which brings us to the more pragmatic topic: establishing your writing process. You must define the time, place, duration, and productivity:

- When (time of day) am I most creative and open?
- Where am I most relaxed and able to focus?
- How much time will I be able to devote to writing each day or week?
- What do I accomplish in that time?

Knowing the above points will enable you to write effectively and consistently. For example, some writers are better in the early morning, and some like to write in odd places, like their cars or bathroom—don't laugh, it happens. It's all about knowing what works best for you.

Now, for new writers, this may be unknown. Finding the time and place that best suits you may take some trial and error. Knowing when your mind is at its most creative will help. For example, if you fall asleep in front of the television after dinner, don't fool yourself into thinking this is an excellent time to write. You won't change your habits that quickly. Yet, if the early morning is when you have the most unencumbered mind and energy, that would be a great place to start.

As for the "where": If you struggle to focus, don't try and write in the kitchen where people are in and out, or you are distracted to take breaks for a drink or snack. We hear it all the time, "Well, I start to write, and then I think, 'let me throw in some laundry,' or 'should I run a quick errand then come back to this?'" Distractions are the writer's most significant issue, so you won't be alone. But you do need to determine how to reduce or eliminate anything that steals your attention.

As for the amount of time and usable content you produce, this will vary. For new writers, understand that some days you will be more productive than others. It's like anything else in that no two days are the same. So once you better understand how long you can write without interruption, and how much of what you write moves you closer to completing your draft, we suggest you return to your outline to validate or adjust your "due dates" or goals—"the more you know" situation.

Again, always give yourself some wiggle room. Know that as long as you are moving forward, you will reach your goal.

 LESSON FOUR ASSIGNMENT:

Use the knowledge you have now and answer the questions below. As explained above, this will be an iterative process of figuring out what works, even for those who think they know.
Writing your memoir is intensely personal, and you will need the space and mindset to be effective. Address the questions below to create a baseline and then go back and adjust if necessary:

1. **Where will you write?**

_____
_____
_____
_____

2. **When will you write?**

_____
_____
_____
_____

3. **How long will you write each day or week?**

4. **How much content will you produce during that time?** (Will you draft a chapter in four hours over a week? Or will it take you six hours to draft half a chapter?) No judgment here…it varies for everyone!

Note: For the novice writer, this lesson and your answers will be more fluid until you learn what works for you. The purpose is to get you to think about how you will approach the process, not to establish absolutes. Any seasoned writer will attest to some days being highly fruitful and others being a total waste—the nature of the process.

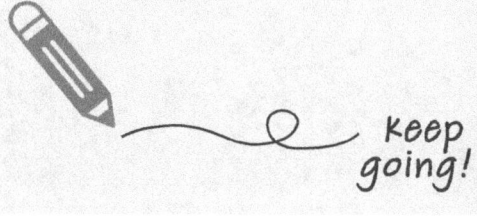

Lesson Five
Begin Writing

About to learn his fate, the author of *The Master Plan*, Chris Wilson, had one last chance to plea to the judge. So, as he stood before the court, he recounted:

"I took a deep breath. This was it. My life in a moment. My fate in a stranger's hands. My last chance, or I would die in a prison cell thirty, forty, fifty years in the future, an old man slurping watery farina from a plastic bowl. And yet I felt calm. I knew what I had to do.

'Your Honor,' I said. 'I want to tell you the truth.'"

These are the final lines of the opening chapter in one of the most riveting memoirs we've read, *The Master Plan*, by Chris Wilson. The judge pauses, and the chapter ends. Flipping the page to the next chapter, you are immediately transported to learn Chris' backstory. The author crafts a tale that weaves the past and present in a way that has you feeling some emotion with each turn of the page: sadness, anger, frustration, disgust, and hope. Not only does the writer hook you from the start—you have to know what happens—but he also crafts his words to show you what he's thinking and feeling in every scene.

Wilson beautifully delivers his story to the reader, and that's precisely what you will do if you follow our guide. Your prep work should be completed now, so let's put that pen to paper or your fingers on the keyboard.

 OBJECTIVE: Put pen to paper and your fingers on the keyboard to produce your first draft.

In this stage, you will focus on writing your story in draft form. Step one: Sit down and use the outline to guide you topic-wise. Step two will be to refamiliarize yourself with the elements below (some previously discussed at a high level) that must be found within your writing:

- **It must be genuine and honest.**
- **Write like a novel.**
- **Show, don't tell.**
- **Write in the first person.**

- **Keep a good pace.**
  - Use metaphors or flashbacks to keep the interest going.
  - Avoid detail that doesn't contribute to the story.
- **Avoid naming others and change identifying details.**
- **Avoid bragging.**
- **Avoid preaching.**

Genuine and Honest

Frequently, this is where our goals and motivations fizzle out. Although we want to bring our story to light, we pull back when it comes to painting the true picture. It's not an uncommon hurdle. Some get past it, others do not, and their memoirs suffer.

We had a client; let's call her Shari. Shari wanted to write a memoir about her troubled past, including her poor choices. Needless to say, she asked us to ghostwrite it for her. She loved the outline and was ready to go. We sat down for our first meeting to interview her before we started. Shari willingly shared every detail of her dysfunctional early twenties.

But, when Shari read the completed chapter one, she called us and said, "I love it, but we can't use it!"

"Why?" We asked.

"I didn't want all that information in there. It makes me look bad," she said.

Essentially, we had written based on the outline and the details she gave us during the interview. Yes, her story popped, and it hooked the reader. Shari agreed with all those facts; however, when she saw the reality of her life on paper, she recoiled. This was when we explained that she didn't have to write her memoir. But if she wanted to do it, she should show all the parts of who she was to contrast against who she is—conveying her story and message in a way that resonates with the reader.

Shari took a break and then came back to us a month later, saying, "Ok, I get what you're saying, and it's important for me to tell my story. I'm ready." And ready she was. She let go of her fears of being judged and opted for the truth to create the impactful, inspiring story of someone who changed their life 180 degrees.

If we had continued to write Shari's story and left out the negative aspects of her early adult life and the poor choices she made, would we have delivered an inspiring memoir? No. If she didn't have any negatives from point A to point B, where's the story? So, if you are writing to inspire, there must be something for the reader to feel incentivized by.

Be open and honest about everything. Readers connect with memoirs because there is humanity in them. Humans err. No one relates to perfectionism.

Also, writing your story can be cathartic, whether it's your goal or not. But healing doesn't happen without reliving some challenging moments. If you are not ready to relive the tough stuff, you aren't prepared to write your memoir. At least not a memoir that will affect the reader.

Additionally, if you are concerned about revealing something that may harm someone in your life, we suggest you speak with them or not name them. We don't suggest you use anything that could result in losing people in your life or causing you to end up in court. No memoir is worth that! However, along those lines, if you are out for revenge and don't care whom you hurt, we ask you to rethink it. We never recommend revenge as a goal in writing your story. It may feel good initially, but it could open you up to legal battles and emotional strife.

That said, your memoir should take the reader on a journey with you, as seen through your eyes—without calling out others specifically—where the reader can connect with you and your challenge while seeing growth at the end. Let the reader relive your journey and feel your emotions. It's not about blame or judgment but allowing the reader to gain something from your story.

Write Like a Novel

Writing like a novel refers to your ability to write with the elements of capturing and keeping the reader's interest, authenticity, showing vs. telling with good pace and flow; your content will come alive to the reader in a way that the read unfolds like a blockbuster movie or a bestselling work of fiction.

Show, Don't Tell

Your content should not be a narrative of you droning on about every detail of what occurred in your life. So avoid writing something that reads like, "this happened, then that happened" —that style is called "telling." When you state what happened, it will end flat with the reader and cause them to shut the book. Make the reader get involved in the story by showing events and situations.

"Showing" entails using dialogue, both internal (thoughts) and external (conversations), and the five senses (look, sound, taste, feel, and smell). We also suggest sprinkling metaphors, flashbacks, and intermittent hooks to draw the reader in further.

For example, let's say you write an inspirational but humorous book about improving your golf game. Initially, you want to write about how bad your game was, highlighting how it made you lose your cool. Below demonstrates showing vs. telling:

If you are telling, you might write: *I was frustrated with my golf game.* Does that impact you, as the reader, in any way? Do you feel connected with the author? On some level, maybe, at best.

But if you write: *My swing barrelled down on the ball and caught the toe of my club, sending the ball soaring toward the fescue and into the mess of trees lining the 10th hole on the mountain course—a course where you are either hitting straight down or straight up. Not that one direction made much difference to me that day. My swing was off, my body couldn't seem to align with my mind, and after losing 10 of the 12 balls I brought with me, I decided to cool off and walk to my opponents' balls in the middle of the fairway.*

I motioned to my competitors in the cart to move forward as I continued on, muttering to myself, 'I hate this f***ing game!' But when I looked up, the cart with my two kids in it looked over at me, my eldest with his eyes bulging and my youngest covering his mouth to suppress his laughter. My eldest yelled, "Mom, you ok?" My youngest let the giggles fly seeing my face and said, "It's ok, Mom. Dad says a lot worse."

Do you see how showing drastically alters the reader's ability to connect with you and your struggles? Essentially, using the elements of thoughts, humor, or visualization conveys a more engaging message. This enables the reader to relate to you on a deeper level—it humanizes you. Once the reader connects with you and your story, you can grab and hold their interest for the whole story as long as you maintain this approach.

Write in the First Person

This is your memoir, so you are the narrator and the protagonist; write in your voice from your perspective. As with any novel, you will want the reader to connect with the main character, you. This will keep the reader engaged in your story.

If you are genuine and honest, as discussed, you will be able to connect with the target reader. However, if you come off as unbelievable, for example, the reader will fail to make that connection with you as the protagonist. You don't have to be perfect, just open and vulnerable; you want the target reader to see themselves in you.

Good Pace and Flow

Pace is all about the rate at which your story progresses. Flow is how all the aspects interact to tell a cohesive and understandable story.

So, for example, have you ever watched the movie *American Pie?* Well, if you haven't, there is one character who is a geeky teen, Michelle, who drones on and on about her experiences at band camp. Michelle starts every other sentence, "And this one time, at band camp...." This constant reiterating of irrelevant facts leaves the other characters to roll their eyes and

think, *Get to the point!* So, if your readers have that reaction, then your pace is too slow.

If you include information that doesn't relate to the message, goes off on a tangent with no point, or keeps repeating something that neither adds nor moves the story along, your pace will be too slow. So take the following into consideration:

- Do not include information you enjoy that has no connection to the theme.
- Create intermittent smaller hooks to engross the reader in your journey.
- Don't get mired down in details that have no point in the story.

We've reviewed a memoir from a client we will call Jason. Jason discussed the same content over and over about events not connected with his story. He assumed he was adding depth with details. However, he failed to see that more isn't always better. For example, he shared moments that deviated away from his message completely and didn't support his story. Although the side stories were entertaining, they derailed the impact of his theme for the reader and caused confusion.

As for your memoir's flow, we are referring to how the content reads from sentence to sentence, paragraph to paragraph, and chapter to chapter. Remember, you want to keep a good pace but want the story to make sense to the reader. You must supply enough details and link content to deliver a cohesive and enticing story. This can be a delicate balancing act, and often, you will identify these areas in the editing process rather than in the first draft.

So, regarding flow, have you ever had that relative or friend that talks incessantly and says nothing because they jump from topic to topic and you can't follow what they say? If so, then you know what it means to have a "flow" issue.

Therefore, in terms of pace and flow, when you edit, try to read the manuscript as if you didn't know the story at all. I know that may sound impossible, but try. If it doesn't work, we suggest you seek beta readers, a writing group, a developmental editor, or a writing consultant to give you feedback. We will discuss these avenues later during the editing process.

Avoid Naming Others

We caution anyone against using their memoir to shame others who may have wronged you. Stick to your personal account and avoid judgment. To avoid hurt feelings or an unnecessary lawsuit, change the locations, years, gender, offenses, or other defining characteristics. Basically, change anything that is a personal identifier.

Avoid Bragging or Preaching

Bragging refers to content that goes on and on about how great you are; don't do it. Remember this: Your reader wants to learn, connect, and be entertained. This is not to say that if you overcame a huge obstacle, you can't celebrate it in your story. In fact, we encourage you to do so as it brings your story full circle, and the reader wants to see that. But celebrating a win after a long struggle is NOT droning on about your greatness. When you tell your story honestly, with all the good and bad that happens, you can deliver a humble but proud celebratory win at the end, and the reader will want to celebrate with you.

Also avoid preaching. Preaching is a steady stream of "you must do this, and you must do that" content. It's a surefire way to have your book tossed aside.

Summary

Ultimately, good writers are great readers. So, if you are stuck about how to start or continue, refer to the list of must-read memoirs provided at the end of this book.

The most critical point to repeat to yourself in this process is:
Only those who finish can be published!

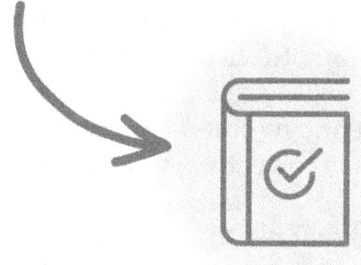

LESSON 5 ASSIGNMENT:

- Using the outline, start by writing your introduction and continue chapter by chapter, being mindful of your completion dates.
- Remind yourself this is a draft and that perfection should never be considered. It's about getting the base information down.
- If you are struggling with something and need to talk it through, use the link and reach out. We are available to help you! A quick consultation will often solve your writer's block and get you started again.
- Stick to your schedule. But if you need someone to hold you accountable, we also offer that service.
- The first draft is to get all your points down. The clean-up and final drafts happen when you self-edit in the next step.

Notes:

scan code to go to our website contact page

Lesson Six
Self-Edit

> "This is not a traditional memoir. Yes I tell stories from the past, but I have no interest in nostalgia, sentimentality, or the retirement most memoirs require…This is an approach book. I am here to tell stories, insights, and philosophies that can be objectively understood, and if you choose, subjectively adopted…" – Matthew McConaughey, Greenlights

 OBJECTIVE: To fine-tune or clean up the messy first draft; every writer's first draft is messy!

Congratulations if you've reached this point;
it means you've finished your draft!
Celebrate!

Then, re-read the quote from the memoir Greenlights above. In the beginning, Matthew clearly states what his memoir is and what it is not. Now, you don't have to do this precisely the same way. However, as the quote indicates, Matthew was in tune with his objective for his memoir. And having read it, we can say he stayed true to his message and tone throughout. You must be as well, especially during the self-edit process, which starts now!

Think of your drafted manuscript as a basecoat of paint where the streaks can show through, and you missed a few spots. You need another "coat" to make it clean and presentable—looking professionally done.

Your first review will focus on a developmental or content edit. This type of edit focuses on the elements/attributes discussed in detail in the previous lesson and are again listed below:

- ☐ **Ensure essential memoir elements are included:**
  - It must be genuine and honest.
  - Show, don't tell.
  - Write in the first person.

- Keep a good pace/flow.
    - Use metaphors or flashbacks to keep the interest going – pace.
    - Avoid detail that doesn't contribute to the story – pace.
    - Identify gaps where the reader could get lost – flow.
    - Identify inconsistencies – flow.
- Write like a novel.
- Avoid naming others and change identifying details.
- Avoid bragging.
- Avoid preaching.

☐ **Initial and intermittent hooks**
☐ **Check for character development and the ability of the reader to connect with the protagonist (you)**
☐ **Clearly communicated theme or message**
☐ **Identify gaps and inconsistencies in the story that don't make sense**
☐ **Assess if readers will connect with the story – real and relatable**
☐ **Assess if the reader will feel the emotions and take the journey with the narrator**
☐ **Identify grammatical errors and punctuation (copy edit)**

After you've developmentally edited, you will review your manuscript to check for spelling errors, punctuation, grammar usage, and overall readability. This is your copy-edit. You can use programs such as Spellcheck or Grammarly to assist you. However, be careful because these programs are often wrong. So, if the suggestions seem odd, double-check using a writer's reference guide or do a Google search. Don't just take what these programs suggest blindly.

Once your file is clean and you are ready to submit it or self-publish, know that a traditional publishing house, if accepted, will put your manuscript through another series of edits and proofreads. However, should you decide to self-publish, you want to ensure the same quality as a mainstream publisher. Therefore, we advise you to use a self-publisher who can provide professional editors and proofreaders to accomplish this.

Notes:
_____
_____
_____
_____
_____
_____

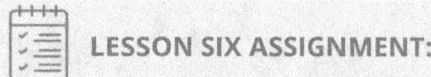 **LESSON SIX ASSIGNMENT:**

Okay, let's clean it up! Follow these steps:

1. **Go back and re-read each of the above-listed attributes defined in detail in lesson six to refamiliarize yourself.**

2. **Read through your completed manuscript as if you are a reader before you edit anything. Avoid making changes during this read. Instead, jot down thoughts or ideas you have on the side.**

3. **Once you've read it through one time, go back and do a developmental, line-by-line self-edit cleaning up for facts while ensuring it meets the following points:**
   - Brutal honesty – don't gloss over things; the reader can tell; reveal characters authentically, showing the good and bad
   - Relatability – the story must be relatable to the reader – readers are reading to relate to their own lives; they need to connect, or you will lose them
   - Show, don't tell – stop being that lecturer of details and show the reader – employ the five senses and dialogue
   - Use flashbacks
   - No vanity, no bragging
   - No boring details that have no point – no minutia
   - Avoid preaching
   - Consider not using real names or personal data
   - No gaps
   - No inconsistencies
   - Assess pacing
   - Check for character development and the likeability of the protagonist
   - Ensure it stays on theme
   - Assess if readers will connect with the story
   - Assess if there are hooks, conflict, and resolution
   - Identify grammatical errors or punctuation

4. **You will probably need to "scrub" or self-edit your manuscript several times to catch everything, and even then, you will miss a few things.** But I caution you to move forward (avoid the merry-go-round of edits) because some writers get stuck in this stage and never progress. Look, anytime you read or re-read something, you will find things to change. Once it meets the above points, it's time to end.

   Remember, an independent editor will look at it before you publish, and we highly recommend one (developmental at least), even before you submit your manuscript to be traditionally published.

5. **Be sure to copy-edit for mechanics.** You can use programs like Grammarly, but be mindful that you only use them as suggestions because these applications are often wrong. Don't get overrun with ensuring you catch everything; aim to make it as clean as possible. You will have professional editors if you traditionally publish, or you should hire them if you self-publish.

6. **We also recommend the following methods to elevate your manuscript:**

    a. Join a writing group where you can share your work weekly and gain valuable feedback from other writers.

    b. Contact us at CLP for beta reads, developmental edits, or coaching.

We highly recommend writing groups or one-on-one sessions with a writing coach for any new writer. These two methods will give you valuable insight, typically chapter-by-chapter, to elevate your skills and reduce your self-editing time.

Also, we recommend beta reads once you've self-edited. A beta read is when your manuscript is read and reviewed by an independent source. This is not an edit. This is not a line-by-line evaluation but an overall critique of your ability to reach the elements described above by someone who is an avid reader of memoirs and preferably has editing and writing experience.

Developmental edits take the beta read to one more level. They go line-by-line, suggesting changes in wording while also making notes in the margin to explain, question, or provide guidance for potential edits.

Writing coaches will assist you at any point during and after the drafting process with any questions or difficulties you have.

Summary

Congratulations on having finished all the steps in this workbook! So what are the next steps? The answer depends on where you are in the writing process and your goals. Understand that the purpose of this workbook was to guide you on how to write a "must-read" memoir. We did not go into publication options as those are more fluid topics. So, if you've completed your manuscript, all you need to do is scan the QR code link here and contact us for a complimentary consultation with no sales pitch or obligation. We are here to guide you through the next steps in a way that makes sense!

scan code to go to our website contact page

Bonus
"Unstuck" Yourself!

No matter what you are writing, there may come a time when you hit that proverbial wall and have no idea where to go. Writer's block is real! So, there are some **tricks and tactics that we suggest to get back on track and write a steady stream in no time:**

- Step away – Put some distance between you and your memoir.
- Read – Read other memoirs similar to yours. This is about inciting motivation and ideas.
- Know where you are at your most creative and maximize it.
- Get outside your writing area and see others.
- Do something you love.
- Revisit your outline, notes, and photos.
- Revisit a place to be discussed in your memoir.
- Speak to someone from your past that knew your story.
- Find that quiet place to reflect.

Step Away

When you close your computer or put down your pen, whichever way you write, sometimes the best way to get "unstuck" with your writing is to give yourself distance. Forcing yourself to stay at it and write will only make matters worse. More often than not, you will want to change what you've written the next day. We've all been there, and it's never the answer to producing a quality product.

The question many may have is how long do you walk away from something. The answer is it varies based on you. Maybe it's an hour, a day, or several days. It shouldn't be too long because you must reacclimate yourself to where you stopped. But, sometimes, even a quick stroll to the kitchen for a glass of water will solve the issue; other times, you may need a night to sleep on it.

Read

This trick almost always works for us. Why? Holding someone else's book makes you realize if they can deliver, so can you. And it also shows different approaches to delivering a story. Often, reading will ignite a spark and give you the clarity you want.

Know Where and When You Are Most Creative

There is always a time and place during the day when anyone is most open to processing ideas. Often, it elicits funny responses when we ask: Where do you do your best thinking? Some of the answers we've had are showering, driving, exercising, church, meditation, grocery shopping, scrolling through social media, and so on. The point is whenever your mind is the least burdened, you will be the most open to ideas. So, know when that is, and create that experience to allow for a refresh and reset.

Get Outside Your Writing Area and See Others

Conversations with others can be cathartic and ease your blockage when it comes to writing. You don't necessarily have to talk about anything specific; often, listening is the best medicine here. The point is to get your mind off what you're trying to write so that when you return, it's like a reset or starting with a clean slate.

Do Something You Love

Again, this is not unlike the above suggestion in that it acts as a distraction to free your mind.

Revisit Your Outline, Photos, or a Place Involved in Your Story

Any of these three will remind you of your goal, the experience you are trying to write about, or reignite feelings, smells, or emotions of the event.

Speak to Someone from Your Past

Just like a photo or piece of memorabilia will spark that creativity, so will having a conversation with someone who knows about your experience. This might even be someone who went through it with you or with whom you shared your story. This communication will allow you to verbalize what you're trying to get out on paper. Perhaps this individual will remind you of something you forgot or even give you an idea of how to proceed.

Find a Quiet Place and Reflect

This works better for some than others. Essentially, it goes back to knowing what you need individually to relax your mind enough to allow room for creative thinking. For some, this could mean going to the beach, taking a meditation class, walking, or fishing. It's individualistic.

> "I don't sit around waiting for passion to strike me. I keep working steadily, because I believe it is our privilege as humans to keep making things. Most of all, I keep working because I trust that creativity is always trying to find me, even when I have lost sight of it." –Elizabeth Gilbert

All the above suggestions basically focus on your ability to open your mind and let other ideas in, whether from others through conversation or through reading. Also, remember to have a phone, notepad, or computer ready when creativity flows; the writing process can be serendipitous, so be prepared to capture your thoughts when they happen.

Now, if all else fails, none of these ideas work, and you are still stuck, reach out to us for a consultation to get you back on track and writing again.

scan code to go to our website contact page

Memoir Recommendations

Maybe You Should Talk to Someone	Lori Gottlieb
Life After Suicide	Jennifer Ashton, M.D.
The Master Plan	Chris Wilson
The Way I Heard It	Mike Rowe
Fail Until You Don't	Bobby Bones
Wild Game: My Mother, Her Lover, and Me	Adrienne Brodeur
High Achiever	Tiffany Jenkins
Smacked	Eilene Zimmerman
The Middle Place	Kelly Corrigan

Notes: